Faithful Servant Series
Meditations for Choir Members

Faithful Servant Series
Meditations for Choir Members

Nancy Roth
Christopher L. Webber, Series Editor

MOREHOUSE PUBLISHING

Morehouse Publishing
P.O. Box 1321
Harrisburg, PA 17105
Morehouse Publishing is a division of The Morehouse Group.

Library of Congress Cataloging-in-Publication Data

Roth, Nancy, 1936–
   Meditations for choir members / Nancy Roth.
      p.   cm. — (Faithful servant series)
   Includes bibliographical references.
   ISBN 0-8192-1779-4 (paper)
   1. Choirs (Music)—Prayer-books and devotions—English.
2. Episcopal Church—Prayer-books and devotions—English.
I. Title. II. Series.
BV4596.C48R68 1999
242'.69—dc21   98-55964
                                                   CIP

Passages marked BCP are from The Book of Common Prayer.

Hymn lyrics are from *The Hymnal 1982*, copyright ©1985 by The Church Pension Fund.

Printed in the United States of America

Cover design by Corey Kent

To the choir of the Church of St. James the Less,
Scarsdale, New York—
our extended family for thirty-three years

I wish to acknowledge my helpful "first editor"—
my husband, Bob—who read each meditation
and offered helpful comments; my friend Steven
Plank, who did likewise; and Debra Farrington,
my editor at Morehouse Publishing, with whom
it has been a pleasure to work.

Contents

———— "You Were Chosen" ————

Were you chosen to read this book? Perhaps it was given to you in a public ceremony or maybe it was handed to you with a quiet "you might like to look at this." Maybe, on the other hand, it reached out to you in a bookstore and said, "Buy me!" Many books choose us in such ways and this book is likelier to have done so than most. But however this book came to you, it almost certainly happened because you have also been chosen for a ministry in the church or for church membership. Perhaps you hadn't considered this as being chosen; you thought you decided for yourself. But no, you were chosen. God acted first, and now you are where you are because God took that initiative.

God acts first—the Bible is very clear about that and God acts to choose us because God loves us. And who is this God who seeks us in so many ways, who calls us from our familiar and comfortable places and moves us into new parishes and new roles? Christians have been seeking answers to that question for a long time.

Part of the answer can be found within the church. We come to know God better by serving as church members and in church ministries. God is present with us and in others all around us as we worship and serve. But there is always more, and God never forces a way into our hearts. Rather, God waits for us to be quiet and open to a deeper relationship.

And that's what this book is about. This is not simply a book to read but to use, in the hope that you will set aside some time every day for prayer and the Bible—and for this book. So give yourself time not only to read but to consider, to think about, to meditate on what you have read. The writers of these short meditations have been where you are, thought about their experiences deeply, and come to know God better. Our prayer is that through their words and experience and your reflection on them, you will continue to grow in knowledge and love— and faithful service—of this loving, seeking God.

— Christopher L. Webber
   Series Editor

Introduction

My introduction to many of the good things of life has been through singing in church choirs. When I was in kindergarten, my parents, who yet had no church affiliation, took me to the local Episcopal Sunday school; my first impression of it was of children just my size, decked out in bright red choir robes. *I* wanted to wear a robe like that. Our choir was conducted by a soft-spoken lady who always wore a red hat to match our vestments and told us about Jesus while she taught us our songs.

When, midway through elementary school, I graduated from the red to the blue choir, I found myself in an entirely different world. Heavy hymnals were thrust into our hands, and I was confused by the necessity to sing words that didn't go down the page properly, like my books in school, but inexplicably made great leaps over other lines of words. In addition to that challenge, I found that, although I had already learned to read piano music, singing the right notes rather than just playing them was something else altogether. Gradually, during that year, I learned to sing from the printed page.

At the age of twelve, I graduated to a choir vested in black and white, and encountered my first and only terrifying choirmaster. He was a well-known choral director who commuted from New York City to direct us. Our parents were proud that we sang under him, believing that we would learn so much about vocal production that we would never need voice lessons. And we did learn, out of fear, for he was notorious for hurling hymnals across the piano when frustration and a quick temper got the better of him.

I continued to sing in the choir through high school, when one of the challenges was to deal with a frail alto who had a propensity for fainting, and through college, where the choir was led by a succession of organ students who were readying themselves for a choirmaster's life in the world outside. And then, toward the end of my senior year, came a telephone call from my ebullient hometown rector, who, it turned out, had the gift of prophecy. "Nancy, I have just hired your future husband." Before the year was out, my tie with the choir director, who had accepted a very self-conscious soprano into the parish choir, was made permanent in a marriage liturgy. The choir sang, of course, with a guest organist in the organ loft.

Our subsequent lives and dinner conversations have often revolved around that amazing and sometimes mystifying group called "the choir" and its place in parish life and worship. We have lived through the publication of the 1979 Book of Common Prayer and its inevitable companion, *The Hymnal 1982*, with all the discussions about the role of music in liturgy that surrounded those publications. We have lived through the various rectors, vestries, and vocal parishioners who either understood what the choir was about or didn't understand at all. We have lived with the choir through warm friendships and through personality conflicts, through illnesses and deaths and marriages and babies. We were, for better or for worse, for thirty-three years, part of the family made up of people who were willing to give of their time and their talents to enhance the worship of our parish church, and they were part of ours.

Since ordination, I have moved to a different place in the chancel. But the years spent in the choir stalls initiated for me the spiritual bond between song and prayer, and I continue to find that bond a rich source of meditation. My work has taken me to many different churches, from Trinity Church, Wall Street, with all of its professional musical resources, to struggling rural churches without any resource but the good will of a few parishioners who can carry a tune. As a result, my experience of church music has broadened and deepened. I hope that this volume of reflections on what it means to be a choir member will resonate with you, who give your gift of song—along with "the whole company of heaven"—to enhance the worship of our God.

Rests

In returning and rest you shall be saved; in quietness and in trust shall be your strength.

(Isaiah 30:15)

One of the more embarrassing things that can happen to a choir singer is to sing an unintentional solo during a rest. The zigzag markings in our scores, which denote an eighth rest or a quarter rest, or the black rectangles perched on top of or hanging below a line in the staff mean that we are supposed to keep quiet.

Rests—those intervals of silence between notes—are, some think, among the most important elements of music. Like a great actor's sense of timing, a rest helps accentuate the meaning of the sounds we sing. A rest helps us to make transitions, as, for example, in the breathing space that experienced organists give their congregations between stanzas of a hymn.

It has been said that one of the most important moments in the history of music is the rest between *et supultus est* ("and was buried") and *et resurrexit* ("and rose again") in Bach's B-minor Mass, giving the listener a moment to experience the empty silence of the tomb on Holy Saturday. A rest helps us absorb the notes that have gone before—the somberness of Good Friday—and prepares us for the exultation to follow.

In our daily lives, rests also help us to make transitions. They are the reflective times in which we pause for a moment in order to gain perspective on what went before and what will follow. Rests help us to take time out from *doing*, in order to experience *being*. They are the meditative times during which we inhale the clear fresh air of prayer, which breathes life into our activities. They give us an opportunity to think about things.

In complying with a musical notation of a rest, we are honoring the composer's intentions. In allowing ourselves moments of quiet in our lives, we are responding to the invitation of the world's Composer to keep the Sabbath: a time when a devout Jew or a wise Christian calls a halt to ceaseless activity in order to rest and to be restored. Our lives are hallowed by those times of stillness when we pause to keep silence before the mystery of God. Our rests, of whatever duration, give us an opportunity to seek the meaning of all the moments when we are busily doing.

The Sabbath times that give meaning to our activities can be sought in many ways: through a walk in the woods, during a weekend retreat, or even within the pages of a book. May this book invite you to a Sabbath time of rest. May it help you to ponder, pray, and find new meaning and new blessings in your music making in the choir.

──────── The Call ────────

Then I heard the voice of the Lord saying, "Whom shall I send, and who will go for us?" And I said, "Here am I; send me!"

(Isaiah 6:8)

Have you ever asked yourself, *Why am I here, in the church choir?* There are probably as many reasons for being in the choir as there are choir members. Somewhere, somehow, sometime, there was a nudge that lured you out to that first choir rehearsal and made you want to stay.

I think that all ministry begins with that nudge. While it may not have seemed so to you at the time, it is quite possible that the nudge was the voice of the Holy Spirit calling you to a special ministry. It is not only ordained clergy who experience a call to ministry. If that were so, the church would be a strange place; it would have no choir, no choir director or organist, no altar guild members, no ushers, no vestries, no acolytes.

When I was in seminary, one of my first assignments was to compile a "spiritual autobiography" that traced the people and the events that drew me toward my vocation. It was a fascinating and humbling experience to look into my past to discover the influences—from the inspiration of a dynamic Sunday school teacher to my experiences as a mother and wife—that finally guided me to begin training for ordination.

I have a "choir autobiography" as well, which you probably have read in the introduction to this volume. I expect that you have one, too. Somehow, from your growing-up years onward, seeds were sown that influenced your decision to sing today in the church choir.

Who, or what, was part of your path to the choir? Was there a beloved music teacher or an organist whom you admired? Was there a particular choral composition that you loved and wanted to sing? Did you hear an excellent choir and want to be part of such a sound?

Think of all the ways God calls us. They are not usually obvious ways. God speaks to us through nudges, through people, events, and the small and subtle things in life. If you sing in the church choir, God called you—and you accepted the call—to the ministry of music. God was there, all along, guiding you gently toward this destination.

Gifts

Now there are varieties of gifts, but the same Spirit; and there are varieties of services, but the same LORD; and there are varieties of activities, but it is the same God who activates all of them in everyone. To each is given the manifestation of the Spirit for the common good.

(1 Corinthians 12:4–7)

Gifts. What a magical word this was when I was a child! It evoked the excitement of Christmas and birthdays, with mysterious packages wrapped in bright paper, whose ribbons I eagerly untied in order to discover what was inside.

Gifts also made me think of the wonderful secret things I made in school to give to my family, from the clay print of my hand that I made in kindergarten to the more skilled crafts of later elementary school: a wooden stake shaped like a daisy for my mother's garden, and a painted and glazed clay lion for my father. Waiting breathlessly as my family opened these gifts, wrapped in tissue custom-printed by a potato carved in the shape of a Christmas tree, I began to discover the wisdom of the words I heard almost every Sunday in church before the offering: "It is more blessed to give than to receive."

How grateful I am that God has given us such a simple route to happiness: the gift of being able to give! Not merely handprints and garden stakes and clay lions, but, most of all, the gifts of our personalities and talents: the skills we have and the things we love to do.

We may sometimes fail to give our gifts. We may have what we think is good reason for neglecting them: perhaps we are so busy with work or family obligations that we think spending time on something we enjoy is selfish. But a surprising thing happens when we acknowledge that God's creative imagination placed a special talent in us; when we discover our personal "handprint" in terms of what we love to do, we are also discovering the unique self God imagined us to be.

If you are in the choir, you probably love to create music—or at least you want to try. Perhaps you sing your favorite hymns in the shower and hum them in the car as you drive to work. You may have found that listening to a great piece of music on the radio or at a concert brings you closer to God. Music is your gift, a way God has given you of drawing close to the holy. In the choir, you add your gift to those of the other singers in order to enhance the worship of the entire church family. You share with others something that you love—your handprint of music—and, in giving that gift, you receive the joy of being entirely yourself as well.

——— Harmony ———

Indeed, the body does not consist of one member but of many....
If the whole body were an eye, where would the hearing be? If the
whole body were hearing, where would the sense of smell be? But
as it is, God arranged the members in the body, each one of them,
as he chose.

(1 Corinthians 12:14, 17–18)

I've always loved contemplating stained-glass windows from the van-
tage point of the choir stalls. I marvel at the way the juxtaposition of
small odd-shaped pieces of glass can miraculously become a picture
glowing with light. It is, after all, only glass, with a bit of lead and sol-
der holding the pieces in place. But once together, it is a wondrous
thing, glowing with light.

Perhaps if St. Paul had known about stained-glass windows, he
would have included them among his analogies for the Christian
community. Perhaps he would have said that each function—choir
singer, priest, chalice bearer, altar guild or vestry member—was like a

piece of glass tinted blue, red, green, white, or yellow. Paul would have celebrated all those colors. He would have told us that church communities, like the design of our bodies and the art of stained glass, benefit from variety.

This variety results from the color and shape of our personalities and talents. In order to best serve God, we do well to offer those gifts in which we have the most skill—to acknowledge that we are blue, yellow, green, or red, and not to try to become a color foreign to our native hue.

For someone who cannot match tones to sing in the choir, for example, could be as jarring as if red glass were used for the fleece of the lamb cradled in the Good Shepherd's arms. Each color has its role: choir members should respect those with other gifts, the other colors of the rainbow. A physicist would tell us that the source of a stained-glass window's sparkle is the interplay of the entire spectrum, creating subtle harmonies like those in the music we sing.

A stained-glass window is nothing without light. Medieval philosophers compared the light shining through the glorious windows of their era to the grace of God. Whatever our talents, we do not serve the community without that grace. Like the glass transformed by sunlight, we are meant to be translucent to the grace shining through us. Our translucence becomes even more brilliant when we recognize the translucence of others in the church who serve in different ways. Together with us, they create the pattern to which our special gifts lead us, welcoming and sharing God's light.

Breath

Then the LORD God formed man from the dust of the ground, and breathed into his nostrils the breath of life; and the man became a living being.

(Genesis 2:7)

In the second chapter of Genesis, God is pictured as a sculptor who takes clay from the earth, fashions a human form, and breathes life into it. Our ancestors who told that profoundly theological creation story knew that breath is life, and that it is a gift from our Creator. The word they used for God's life-breath is *ruach*, which is pronounced with an appropriate "swoosh" of breath on the final syllable. Both in the Greek equivalent, *pneuma*, and the Latin, *spiritus*, the word suggests the life-giving, creative breath of God.

Notice your breath at this moment. It is probably slow and regular, as you spend this quiet time with God. But think of the other ways you breathe during a typical day: panting as you make a fast trip to the grocery store, gasping when you think you've gotten a parking ticket, sighing in relief when you discover it is just an advertising flier tucked under your windshield wiper.

Our breathing tells us a great deal about our relationship with God, the source of our life-breath. When we pause too long in our breathing, our lungs ache for oxygen and compel us to inhale. Just as our need for oxygen causes us to breathe, so our need for God reminds us to pray. Often that reminder takes the form of a sense of yearning or emptiness, as if we are waiting for the next inhalation.

When I think about Genesis 2:7, I realize that life-breath fills my whole body, not merely my lungs. Oxygen is carried by the bloodstream to renew *all* of me, from the top of my head to the end of my toes. The more oxygen I can take in with each breath, the more there is to go around. So I try to sit or stand in such a way that my entire rib cage—front and back—can expand with my inhalations. I try to let my abdomen expand as well, so that my diaphragm can drop, enabling the lungs to fill completely. I imagine my spine reaching toward the sky, supporting all this activity.

And I try to exhale completely—daring to let go, for a moment, all my life-breath—because I know that there will be inevitably another inhalation, and then another exhalation, on and on until the moment I breathe my last. I know that if my lungs are empty, I am making more room for the next breath.

I try to open my whole self to receive God's life and love in the same way. It is sometimes tempting to erect barriers: to hold back some petty resentment or selfish indulgence that I don't want to let go. But God's loving energy wants to renew all of me, not merely the parts of me that I decide to offer for renewal.

The gift of breath is the source of our physical life and a helpful metaphor for our spiritual life. The breath is also, of course, the source of our song. Our song is not ours alone; its origin is in God. When our breath causes our vocal cords to vibrate in producing music, we are, in a sense, giving back that breath to its Source in prayer and in praise.

Body

For you yourself created my inmost parts; you knit me together in my mother's womb. I will thank you, because I am marvelously made.

(Psalm 139:13–14a, BCP)

When I was a little girl singing in church choirs and school choruses, I used to think that I sang with my throat. As I learned a little more about anatomy, I began to realize that my lungs had something to do with the process as well. But now I know that when I sing, I sing not just with my throat and my lungs, but with my whole body.

During my elementary school years, life was full of vigorous physical activity. Jumping rope at recess, climbing the maple tree in our backyard, riding bikes with my friends on our dead-end street, and taking ballet lessons gave me plenty of opportunities to use my muscles and fill my lungs with oxygen.

During my adolescence, however, my days were crammed full with high school classes, homework, and hours of piano practice. Because it was the most sedentary period of my entire life, I remember often feeling overwhelmed with fatigue. My lone exertion, with the exception of swimming in the summer, was the short walk from school to church for Wednesday afternoon junior choir practice. At rehearsal, my throat often felt tight and uncomfortable, and it was difficult to sing the long phrases our demanding choirmaster wanted.

During college I rediscovered how much I enjoyed dance, and I began taking ballet classes again. I noticed a new sense of physical well-being, and, to my surprise, my experience of singing began to change. Secret stolen breaths during the anthem were less necessary, and my new muscle tone made it easier to sit up straight and to support my voice. I will never be a great singer (I don't have the vocal apparatus), but I discovered that being in good physical shape contributes enormously to my making the best use of the voice I do have.

The singer's instrument, the body, needs care and tuning; it is a small universe of interconnected parts. The more I learn about its design, the more I find myself in awe of the God who "knit me together in my mother's womb." I marvel at all the body's systems: the efficiency of the skeleton; the resilience and strength of muscles, tendons, and ligaments; the complexity of the nervous, reproductive, immune, and digestive systems; the perpetual rhythm of heart and breath.

When I think about all this, I feel a sense of wonder coursing through me, from my head to my toes, like another system flowing through my physical self. This wonder generates a song within me, singing from a body resonating with the energy of life: "I will thank you, because I am marvelously made; your works are wonderful, and I know it well."

—————————— Unity ——————————

I ask not only on behalf of these, but also on behalf of those who will believe in me through their word, that they may all be one. As you, Father, are in me and I am in you, may they also be in us, so that the world may believe that you have sent me. The glory that you have given me I have given them, so that they may be one, as we are one.

(John 17:20–22)

In the seventeenth chapter of John's Gospel, Jesus prays that the apostles will mirror the divine unity: "so that they may be one, as we are one." Jesus' disciples would have easily understood oneness, for they lived in a culture where community was a cherished value. The ultimate shame was to be an outcast, which is why Jesus' contemporaries were so scandalized when he consorted with tax collectors and lepers.

In Western industrial society, however, individualism is a higher value than belonging to a community. In education, sports, and business alike, we are urged to compete rather than cooperate. So singing in a choir could be seen as a profoundly countercultural act! When we sing in a choir, we abandon our egocentric desire to stand out; we give up our individuality for a time and become a part of a whole. We may have a voice like Caruso, years of musical education, and the extroverted personality of a born performer. We may be volunteer singers, or we may be professionals hired as section leaders. But that does not matter: we do not come here as soloists, but as choral singers. We come to cooperate.

The music created by the artistry of disparate individuals who have lost themselves—and found themselves—in the act of singing together is one of the wonders of life. For proof, listen to any of the great English cathedral choirs, or to the humblest parish choir that has discovered the joy of singing as one.

When we become one voice, we are reflecting the pattern of the Trinity—our God who is three persons, yet a unity. When a collection of sopranos, altos, tenors, and basses becomes a unity, the results are glorious: "The glory that you have given me I have given them."

When the choir sings, we mirror the Creator's pattern imprinted in the natural world, for interrelationship and interdependence are the way in which the creation works. We also are part of the natural order, yet made in the image of the Trinity. We who call ourselves Christians are meant to become a community, the body of Christ. Perhaps, as our many different voices unite to sing God's praises, those who hear us will realize what that means.

Rehearsal

Therefore let us go on toward perfection.

(Hebrews 6:1)

Whether the choir meets on a week night, on Sunday morning before the service, or both, we need to practice the music we will be singing when the parish community gathers for worship. Rehearsal is often painstaking work and may even sometimes seem tedious. The French word for rehearsal, *répétition*, sometimes seems all too appropriate. In choir practice, we are likely to repeat difficult passages many times in order to master our music.

Commitment to attending rehearsal might mean missing an interesting event or finding a baby-sitter for the children. But if we assume that because we know the music, we don't need to practice, we are thinking as individuals and not as members of a unified body that needs all its parts—every soprano, alto, tenor, and bass—to produce its sound.

Rehearsal reminds us of the integral connection between discipline and freedom. Like the pianist who must practice scales in order to express the music of Chopin or Mozart, and like the ballet dancer who must do barre exercises in class in order to be able to dance "Swan Lake," the choir needs to rehearse in order to gain the freedom to express its art. Even when we have learned an anthem, we have not finished our task. We need to go beyond just singing the notes, and, under the guidance of our director, give expression to the words and the text through variations in dynamics or tempo. Finally, when we have learned an anthem so well that our musicality is no longer self-conscious obedience to the choir director, the music begins to sing through us.

I've often noticed the similarities between rehearsal and prayer. We may be tempted, for a variety of reasons, to skip prayer. Sometimes when we pray, it seems tedious. However, if we persevere, something begins to happen. We may not notice it during our prayer time, but we will notice it in our lives.

For just as rehearsal is not an end in itself but a preparation for singing God's praises in worship, our prayer time is not a goal but a preparation. The goal is what you might call the music of our lives. When we focus on God in prayer, a quiet transformation begins to take place, as if we were learning the notes to a holy life. When we bring our concerns before God in prayer time, we are learning the habit of bringing everything before God as we go about our daily activities. Like choir rehearsal, prayer gives us the freedom to express an art: the art of living fully all the joys and the challenges of life with God.

———————— Worship ————————

Worship the LORD in the beauty of holiness.

(Psalm 29:2b, BCP)

How can I worship when I'm performing? As someone who loves attending quiet early services and joining my Quaker friends in their silent meetings, I've often thought about that question. The first part of the answer, of course, is that we are not performing merely for our fellow human beings. Like Johann Sebastian Bach, who wrote on his manuscripts *Soli Deo Gloria* ("to God alone be glory"), we are singing to glorify God. In doing so, we are contributing, with the best skill we can muster, to the beauty of holiness.

This involves not only our musical leadership, but also our active participation in the congregation's prayers and responses. We need to be thinking ahead, making sure we have the right page in the prayer book. We have to be the ones who know that on the first Sunday in Lent, we must respond "His mercy endures forever" instead of the customary "And blessed be his kingdom, now and forever." It is often up to us to set a confident tone in the Creed and to give voice to the responses in the Prayers of the People, to say nothing of participating with enthusiasm in the congregational role in the Great Thanksgiving. We must be ready for the next hymn, and, if there is a musical setting of the service, we have to prepare to flip those pages back and forth. We must pay attention both to our music and to the choir director as we sing the anthem. So how can we worship?

Perhaps part of the answer lies in expanding our understanding of worship. We gather not as a collection of individuals having private dialogues with God, but as a community. Communities express worship in many different ways, from the silence of Quaker meetings to complex liturgies involving music, speech, incense, candles, vestments, bells, and even dance. In all of these, we are *together*, neither solitary nor passive. The word "liturgy" itself is derived from two Greek words meaning "people" and "work." When we gather on a Sunday morning, worship is our work, and our work is our worship. It is the active offering to God of the community's attentiveness and skill, in adoration and praise.

When we have experienced this unity of work and worship in church, perhaps we can practice it outside as well. We can pray through our action, dedicating our ordinary tasks, as well as our special undertakings, to God. Like Brother Lawrence, the monastery cook, we can "turn the cake that is frying on the pan for love of Him," just as we sing our anthem for love of God. What turns our action into prayer is the same thing that turns our performance into worship: our desire to give God the glory, *Soli Deo Gloria!*

Timbre

The voice of the LORD is a powerful voice; the voice of the LORD is a voice of splendor.

(Psalm 29:4, BCP)

Tone quality, or timbre, gives away who we are. When I pick up the phone, I recognize the voice of family and friends before they identify themselves. When I hear certain singers or instrumentalists on the radio, I do not always need to wait for the announcer to name them. Some birds I know by their song: the liquid trills of the wren sitting on the roof of the birdhouse, the alleluias of the cardinal perched on the highest branch of the oak, the chickadee's merry "chick–a–*dee.*"

"There is nothing on earth that hath not its tone," wrote Martin Luther. "Even the air invisible sings when smitten with a staff."[1] The sound of human voices and the song of a bird are demonstrations of the "air invisible" singing—of vibrations. Thunder and wind, the French horn and the clarinet, the ocean surf and the racing brook, all betray their identity through the quality of the vibration that strikes our ears—those ingeniously convoluted folds designed to receive vibrations and transmit them to the brain. The vibrations we hear, the tone quality, helps us to recognize the world around us.

So how do we recognize the voice of God? Wouldn't it be easy if, indeed, it were always an extraordinary voice of power and splendor, which was guaranteed to capture our attention? An unmistakable voice, like the one hovering above the river Jordan at Jesus' baptism, or knocking the zealous Saul right off his horse?

Instead, for most of us the voice of God is better described by the experience of the prophet Elijah, who heard the Lord not in the wind, the earthquake, or the fire, but in the "sound of sheer silence." In "The Spiritual Canticle," St. John of the Cross wrote of that timbre: My beloved is "the mountains, the solitary wooded valleys, strange islands … silent music."

Silent music. God's voice sings to us through everything. It reverberates through sheer silence and through mountains and valleys and islands and the events that occur in these landscapes. It whispers to us in our solitary prayer. It is the nudge of conscience, the welling up of desire to become what we glimpse we are meant to be.

We hear such music not with the physical ear, but with the ear of an attentive spirit. It is as if Luther's "air invisible" were singing around us and within us, with a timbre that we can identify, if we listen well, as the voice of God. How do we recognize it? We recognize it because it is the voice of unconditional love calling to us. It sings of the goodness of creation, including ourselves. It sings of the splendor of life. It not only sings to us, but also calls us to join in the song.

Coming In

But immediately Jesus spoke to them and said, "Take heart, it is I; do not be afraid." Peter answered him, "LORD, if it is you, command me to come to you on the water." He said, "Come." So Peter got out of the boat, started walking on the water, and came toward Jesus.

(Matthew 14:27–29)

Beginning is difficult. The choir director's arm is raised on the upbeat. You take a breath, ready to sing the first note. Do you dare? What if no one else comes in? What if it is the wrong note? Yet if no one takes the plunge, there will be no music. The choir needs to muster the courage to come in.

If there are professional section leaders or singers with more training than ours, it is tempting to depend on them through perfecting the art of singing a split second after we have heard their voices. But perhaps one day those we regard as the "experts" will have to miss rehearsal, or worse yet, Sunday morning, and we will be on our own. Then we realize that each of us must learn the music, look up from our scores, and be ready to come in.

The many beginnings that occur again and again in our lives can also be difficult. Starting school. The first job. The first day your child goes to preschool or kindergarten. Changing jobs. Moving. Retiring. Bereavement. To make our beginnings, we need courage.

Peter walked on the water of the turbulent Sea of Galilee toward his Master. He took that first impulsive step into the waves because his eyes were on Jesus, who assured him, "Take heart, it is I; do not be afraid."

Perhaps that is the key to our own difficult beginnings. It is Jesus who can give us heart, or *coeur*, the French root of courage. Knowledge that every step of our lives is a step toward him makes it possible to dare to take the first step of all.

Once we have taken it, we will find it much easier to take the next one, and the next. God keeps calling us to reach beyond what we regard as our limitations, whether it be summoning the courage to come in on the first note or walking through one of life's passages.

When the choir director beckons us to sing the first note, we can think of Peter. Whether we are singing or walking on water, we can look beyond ourselves, and, with courage and trust, simply begin.

Therefore we praise you, joining our voices with Angels and Archangels and with all the company of heaven, who for ever sing this hymn to proclaim the glory of your Name: Holy, holy, holy LORD....

(Book of Common Prayer, 362)

In an age when many people feel isolated and alone, our churches attempt to provide the sense of community that is lacking in the world. There are obvious ways to reach for that elusive ideal, but my many years of singing in the choir have taught me that the best way to form community is simply to work together. The choir's sense of being a family grows through its round of rehearsals and services. Social events for the choir do not form the community; rather, they celebrate it. In our church, the annual choir picnic in June is like a Thanksgiving dinner in which all the aunts and uncles and nieces and nephews gather to celebrate what is already a reality: that we are a unit.

We became a community despite my husband's insistence that the time allotted for rehearsal was not for socializing—although I have to admit that it was tempting to whisper the latest family news to my seatmate as we ducked our heads into our choir folders to look for the next anthem. Finally, my husband decided to have a pot of coffee ready before the beginning of rehearsal so that early arrivals could relax and get caught up on the events of the week.

Sometimes the choir even creates a family. Many years ago, I remember noticing that Chuck, a young widower in our bass section, looked more often at Leslie, an alto opposite him, than at the choir director. Their eventual marriage was a celebration for the choir as well; the gift of love had blossomed in our midst.

As in any family, when joy came to some of us, we all shared in it. When suffering came to some of us, we shared in that as well, through both prayers and the offering of practical help in whatever ways we could do so. During the sad months of Chuck's valiant battle against cancer, choir members were faithful visitors and collaborated in hoisting him in his wheelchair up some steep steps to the annual choir picnic, where he played his trombone with the parish jazz ensemble in a final jam session.

Now, eight years and five hundred miles away from that choir family, we still feel connected to them. It is as if community, once established, can never be dissolved. The choir members, both those living and those departed, live within our memories—no, more than our memories, within *us*.

My friend Steven says that when he walks down the aisle with the choir on a Sunday morning, he feels as if he is walking in the company of the Communion of Saints. Later in the worship, of course, we hear the preface to the Sanctus—"Therefore we praise you, joining our voices with Angels and Archangels and with all the company of heaven"—and we realize that Steven is right. Perhaps our experience with the choir community is both a symbol and a foretaste of our communion with all Christians. Singing God's praises with "all the company of heaven," and also with all the company of Christians on earth may just be the most perfect way to find the community we long for.

Listening

It is the same way with lifeless instruments that produce sound, such as the flute or the harp. If they do not give distinct notes, how will anyone know what is being played?

(1 Corinthians 14:7)

Once a little girl named Susi auditioned for my husband's junior choir. She was enthusiastic about singing, but she was only a few notes into "My Country 'tis of Thee" when he realized that she was "Susi one-note": a monotone. Not wanting to turn her down, my husband suggested that Susi meet with me for a few sessions to learn how to match tones, and Susi willingly agreed.

Our sessions were a confirmation of what I'd long believed: most monotones have just never learned how to listen attentively, either to the notes they want to match or to their own voices. We began with one note at a time. I would play it on the piano, sing it, then ask Susi to sing it. Susi's eagerness to be in the choir was matched by her perseverance. And finally, she could match any note within her vocal range.

We next tried matching two notes, one after the other, and Susi conquered that hurdle. We moved on to three notes, then four, then longer melodic patterns. By the end of a couple of months, Susi proudly joined the junior choir.

Listening is the basis of all good music making. It is also the source of a satisfying and holy life. Like Susi, we need to listen both to ourselves and to the world outside ourselves in order to discover whether we are matching tones.

What are the gifts we hold within ourselves? *Listen!* How do we use them in matching the needs of the world around us—in church, at home, in our communities?

What are the stresses and burdens that we carry? *Listen!* We may not even have realized that we were weighed down. We may need to simplify our lives or to ask for help—perhaps from other people and surely from God.

What are the aspects of our lifestyle that are out of tune with our beliefs? *Listen!* We may waste natural resources, while preaching stewardship of the earth. We may spend an inordinate amount of time focused on our business, although we maintain that "our family comes first." We may harbor hatred, while singing of God's love.

What are the ways God is calling us? *Listen!* Perhaps God is calling us to tune ourselves. God is calling us to use all the notes of our unique personalities, to cast our burdens on our Lord, and to discover the freedom of living the truths we profess. God is calling us to contribute the song of our lives to the well-being of the world around us. Perhaps God is calling us to sing a new song, one that we could not even have imagined. The former "Susi one-note" learned to listen not only to the music of the choir, but also to the music of the God whose praises the choir sang. This persevering, eager little girl became the Rev. Susi, singing a new song—and I am not at all surprised.

—————— **Trouble in the Parish** ——————

Why are the nations in an uproar? Why do the peoples mutter empty threats?

(Psalm 2:1, BCP)

Human nature, in the church as well as in "the nations," may cause uproars. Neither clergy nor laity are immune. So sometimes there is trouble in the parish, and sometimes that trouble even makes it difficult to sing. Once in a while, personality conflicts or differences of opinion concerning the music program become the source of the uproar. Occasionally, because of the emotional power of music, the work of the choir can even become a scapegoat, a target for unconscious anger that has its origin in situations totally outside the realm of music.

When discord interrupts the harmony intended for the Christian community, I am reminded of Hildegard of Bingen, a twelfth-century abbess, visionary, writer, and composer, whose works have recently become popular. When Hildegard was an old woman, her abbey was placed under an interdict forbidding all services of worship, because

Hildegard had disobeyed church authorities by burying an excommunicated youth in the church cemetery.

Hildegard knew the power of music: "Sometimes when we hear a song we breathe deeply and sigh. This reminds the prophet that the soul arises from heavenly harmony."[2] In a strongly worded letter, she wrote to the authorities that "closing the mouth of the Church" aided and abetted the work of the Devil. "What about those in the Church who ... impose silence on the singing of God's praise? If on Earth they have committed the wrong of robbing God of the honor of the praise which is God's due, then they can have no fellowship with the praise of the angels in heaven."[3] Her persuasive words eventually convinced her superiors that it was wrong for the music of God's praises to be held ransom because of ecclesiastical controversies.

And it still is wrong. Our worship must continue, despite any troubles caused by personalities and politics. The choir can help both parishioners and staff remember why the church exists: to sing God's praises through our worship and with our lives. By our example, we can remind everybody that "minding our business"—which in our case is the business of singing—is like a life buoy in the turbulence around us.

We can provide stability for others in times of trouble by making sure that God's praises continue. And our own music making can provide an oasis of peace for us. As we focus on learning and perfecting our anthems and hymns, we can forget for a while the troubles in the parish. As we give our attention to doing our best at the task to which we have been called, we will, in ways we cannot even imagine, help to tune the parish once again to the music of God's love.

———————— Trouble in the Choir ————————

Peace I leave with you; my peace I give to you.

(John 14:27a)

Sometimes the peace of the choir is upset by disharmony from within. It can happen for many reasons: musical differences of opinion, jealousy of someone who is given a solo, resentment of paid section leaders, territorialism about a particular seat in the rehearsal room or choir stalls, clashing personalities, or just general orneriness. I remember an alto with a chip on her shoulder who regularly caused one of her colleagues to dissolve into tears. At a time like that, it feels as if the choir is like a grand piano with some strings jangling out of tune.

When I was studying music in college, I took a course in piano technology, in which we were taught how to tune a piano according to equal temperament. First, we matched the note of a single string with the sound of a tuning fork. Then we were supposed to tighten or loosen the strings so that the octaves had a pure, clear tone. That octave was to be divided into twelve equal semitones; for the intervals in between, we were supposed to hear "beats"—subtle pulses in the sound—that indicated those intervals were equally spaced.

Musicians did not always tune this way. In our town, for example, there is a marvelous mean tone organ tuned to a system used in the sixteenth century, in which the octave is divided so that the thirds are also perfectly pure and clear.

Sometimes, we choir members seem to want to invent our own tuning systems, perhaps with an emphasis on an interval of our own choice—where we sit, when we sing, what the rules are. We'd like everything arranged to suit our own temperament. Maybe we'd like to be like that mean tone organ, which is absolutely brilliant in the rendition of certain compositions; the problem is that it literally sets one's teeth on edge in music not suited to it.

Sometimes we forget that equal temperament is the way we sing now. Maybe a choir in trouble is like a piano in which some strings have been pulled too tightly, while others remain overly slack. Some of us may need to "loosen up," yielding our desire for tight control. Some of us may need to "tighten" by refusing to let the foibles of others get under our skin.

Our best remedy is allowing God to tune our hearts to the note that rings throughout Scripture and Christian history, the note called by many names: loving-kindness, compassion, understanding, forgiveness. We each are like instruments that need to be tuned again and again, in order to live in harmony with others. God has given us the means to learn this harmony, through the example—and, more than that, the *presence* in our hearts and communities—of Jesus Christ, whose peace is God's gift to us.

—————— Healing ——————

And the ransomed of the LORD shall return, and come to Zion with singing; everlasting joy shall be upon their heads; they shall obtain joy and gladness, and sorrow and sighing shall flee away.

(Isaiah 35:10)

After the Second Vatican Council, a new abbot was appointed to a Benedictine monastery in the south of France. He made some drastic changes, among them the discontinuation of the plainsong that the monks had been accustomed to singing regularly during their worship throughout the day and night. Soon thereafter the monks became plagued with depression, fatigue, and listlessness. Was this some strange illness? Medical specialists were called in to experiment with the monks' schedules and diets, but they admitted defeat.

Finally, the abbot called on Dr. Alfred Tomatis, a physician who had established a center in Paris for research in the connection between hearing and health. After assessing the situation, Tomatis gave the community a simple prescription: Begin singing again.

The effect was dramatic; within six months, the monks were once again vigorous. Tomatis explained that music actually recharged the monks just as batteries can be recharged: the frequencies of plainsong had not only a psychological effect but a physical one, as the vibrations resonated within the monks' bodies and once again gave them the will to live.

I think that most of us have experienced something of the healing power of music. Perhaps we have felt listless and discovered a surge of energy when we put our favorite CD on the stereo, or we have felt anxious and music has soothed us. We know how it is to be charged by music, as it tunes both our spirits and our bodies.

Western medicine is beginning to call on music's power. The director of a critical care unit in Baltimore reported that, when he played music for his patients, "half an hour of music produced the same effect as ten milligrams of Valium." Music is used in operating theaters to keep the surgeons alert and the patients relaxed. It even has the capacity for social healing: in the city of Edmonton, Canada, Mozart's music piped into the city squares has been found to calm pedestrian traffic and decrease drug dealing.[4]

No less a theologian than Martin Luther considered music a gift of God, as potent as the medicinal herbs that grow in the woodlands and the fields: "Music is an endowment and a gift of God, not a gift of men. It also drives away the devil and makes people cheerful; one forgets all anger, unchasteness, pride, and other vices. I place music next to theology and give it the highest praise."[5]

It is no wonder that the bliss of heaven is usually pictured in terms of singing saints and angels, for music helps us feel whole, bringing into harmony our hearts, our minds, and our bodies. We would do well, when we feel out of sorts, to remember that gift from God, as close as our radio, stereo, or piano—or even our own voices.

Mourning

Jeremiah also uttered a lament for Josiah, and all the singing men and singing women have spoken of Josiah in their laments to this day.

(2 Chronicles 35:25a)

The choir is not merely a setting for music of joy; it is also a place for laments. Three events in particular stand out in my memory.

On Thursday, April 4, 1968, I was delayed in getting to rehearsal. Just as I turned into the church parking lot, I heard on the car radio that Martin Luther King had been shot. I became the bearer of that news to a shocked gathering of singers, who had just at that moment opened their music to the *Nunc Dimittis*—"Now, lettest thou thy servant depart in peace." We decided to sing it in tribute to that faithful servant of God, and I never sing that canticle without thinking of him.

I always associate the Brahms "Requiem" with Arthur, the husband of one of our altos. We sang the "Requiem" shortly after Arthur had died in the recovery room after open heart surgery. In our hearts, that concert was dedicated to his memory, difficult as it was to sing with lumps in our throats.

Then there was Margie, who planned our laments ahead of time. Margie, well along in years by the time my husband became choir director, would often exclaim when she heard a favorite anthem or hymn, "I want this at my funeral!" One day, my husband took her aside: "Are you serious about this? Perhaps we should sit down and plan your funeral music." And so they did just that, with written instructions for the family. When she died a couple of years later, her funeral was a combination of a lament and a celebration custom-designed by the deceased, like a musical funeral banquet.

I think of those psalms called laments and how they enabled the singer to pour out his sorrow to God: "O Lord, I call to you; my Rock, do not be deaf to my cry.... I cry to the Lord with my voice; to the Lord I make loud supplication.... O Lord, my God, my Savior, by day and night I cry to you.... Out of the depths have I called to you, O Lord; Lord, hear my voice."

A psalm enabled Jesus Christ to cry out his agony on the cross: "My God, my God, why have you forsaken me?" These psalms and music like a requiem or the *Nunc Dimittis* can enable us to pour out our sorrow, too. Sadness is a part of human life. The longer we live, the more we realize that loss is an integral part of the human condition. Music can give voice to our mourning and help us toward the healing of our grief, as we share our sadness with God, the bearer of all our pain.

Singing Outside

How could we sing the LORD's song in a foreign land?
(Psalm 137:4)

When the Hebrew people were led away as captives to Babylon, their oppressors taunted them: "Sing us one of the songs of Zion." The exiled Hebrews had no heart to sing; instead, they sat down and wept by the waters of Babylon.

When *we* sing the Lord's song in a foreign land—or even just down the street at a neighboring church—it is quite a different matter. Rather than sitting down and weeping, we are likely to bring new enthusiasm to our music making because of the excitement of singing for people outside our parish.

When my husband was choir director of our church, he, like many organists, moonlit at a synagogue nearby. Each year, in addition to the regular music for Sundays, we would prepare two major works to be sung in concert or during a Sunday service. In many cases, the music (such as Mendelssohn's "Elijah" or Handel's "Judas Maccabeus") was appropriate for use in the synagogue, so the choir would be invited to sing as guests at the Sabbath Eve service. The Jews received us like God's itinerant prophets; we, who sometimes felt like "prophets without honor" in our own church (people sometimes take us for granted), were overwhelmed with the welcome.

But we received much more than a welcome. We received a part of our religious education. Turning the leaves of the Jewish Prayer Book, we realized how very familiar all this was, for the pattern of the daily offices of Morning and Evening Prayer had its origin in early synagogue worship. For a while, we worshipped as Jesus and his disciples had worshipped. We had come back to our roots.

We ventured even farther afield one summer, joining with the choir of the local United Church of Christ for a two-week concert tour of English cathedrals. It was a new experience, even for some inveterate world travelers among us, to contribute something—our repertoire of American music—to the people who welcomed us there. Like a band of pilgrims, we all drew closer. We grew in understanding of a different culture, as we contributed to the worship of each cathedral. And perhaps we helped them grow as well. Upon our arrival in Winchester to sing Evensong, for example, I was amazed to be asked to read the Old Testament Lesson. Because it was well before any English women had been ordained, I felt like a missionary, probably the first female the congregation had ever seen wearing a clerical collar.

When the choir ventures forth from its comfortable parish boundaries, we may feel at first as if we are going into alien territory. But this kind of travel—whether of a few blocks or of several thousand miles—can be a bridge between ourselves and others who are different from us. It is a pilgrimage undertaken in the company of the Spirit, who guides us in furthering the unity of all peoples and urges us on, as we all move toward our common destiny in God.

Children

Let the little children come to me, and do not stop them; for it is to such as these that the kingdom of God belongs.

(Luke 18:16)

A friend of ours, who is editing a hymnal for very young children, says that she envisions a mother (or a father) seated at a piano with a child on her lap, her encircling arms playing the accompaniment.[6] What a wonderful heritage that child will have; experiencing music in an atmosphere of love will make a lifelong impression. When we share the music of our faith with children, it becomes as natural to them as the welcoming comfort of a parent's arms.

I remember my mother singing "Jesus, tender shepherd, hear me/bless thy little lamb tonight/through the darkness be thou near me/keep me safe 'til morning light" each night, as I lay in my warm bed with my eyelids getting heavier and heavier. Curled up safely under the blankets, hearing the reassurance that Jesus would keep me safe, it was easy to relax into sleep. During my childhood years, the fact that Jesus was my "tender shepherd" became etched on my soul, and I, in turn, sang it to our children. I am quite certain that my conviction of God's goodness and love has its roots in those bedtime lullabies.

The love of music, like faith, is contagious. Children love to imitate the adults who surround them. One evening, our alto and tenor section leaders, Mary and Mukund, who were fairly new parents of Davidas, came to rehearsal with news of their child's latest accomplishment. He had spotted a piece of their choir music, picked it up, and begun to sing, although he had not yet spoken his first word.

Listen to an infant prattle or young children singing and chanting as they play. Exploring sound is one way they discover the wonders of the world into which they have been born. The childhood years full of the freshness of wonder are fleeting; too soon they will become grown-up and blasé.

But is it truly grown-up to take all this sound around us for granted? Jesus taught us *not* to take childhood for granted or to dismiss it as something we grow out of. Instead, we are to receive his kingdom as a little child. When he gathered the little ones around him despite the objections of his disciples, he was surrounded by hearts extraordinarily open to his message of love.

Just as it is important to pass on our music and our faith to the children we know, we can receive this gift of openness from them in turn. We can imitate them, learning to hear once again with the eager ears of childhood, to sing with their enthusiasm, and to open our hearts to our Lord—"for it is to such as these that the kingdom of God belongs."

——— Nature's Song ———

The flowers appear on the earth; the time of singing has come, and the voice of the turtledove is heard in our land.

(Song of Solomon 2:12)

We humans are not the earth's only singers. We are part of a larger symphony, the music of all creation. And we can delight in this symphony, as God surely does, when we take time to listen. Wherever we are—in forest, jungle, or desert, or on mountains or plains—nature sings. The wolf, the tiger, the elephant, the mountain lion, the eagle, all have their parts in the chorus.

If I lived by the ocean, nature's music would be sung against the ground bass of the surf, thundering perpetually like a great thirty-two-foot organ pipe. If I were able to live under the ocean, I would hear the amazing cadenzas sung by our close cousins, the whales and dolphins.

But we don't have to go to exotic places to hear the infinite musical variety of nature. Even in the city, the sounds of some of God's smallest creatures can be heard. Pigeons in the square, crickets in the park, the wind whistling down the avenues, rain splashing the sidewalks—all are part of the symphony.

The writer of the Song of Solomon reminds us to listen for the passage of the seasons. "Now the winter is past, the rain is over and gone. The flowers appear on the earth; the time of singing has come, and the voice of the turtledove is heard in our land." Where I live, the rain is not over and gone in the spring, fortunately for the chorus of frogs who begin their opera season on the first warm evening. During the daytime, I work in the garden to the jubilant accompaniment of the spring songs of cardinals, robins, goldfinches, song sparrows, and the voice of the mourning dove, punctuated by the occasional squawks of blue jays and blackbirds.

In high summer and autumn the insects begin their chorus, buzzing, whining, and whirring. It is a wonder on a summer night to go out with a flashlight to try to track down the source of all this din, and to discover a tiny winged musician, no bigger than my smallest fingernail.

In winter, the world of nature is quieter, in keeping with the waiting silence of the season. But as in all other seasons, the wind sings its song—running the gamut from pianissimo to fortissimo. Rain, sleet, hail, and snow make their distinctive sounds on our roof. Trees creak, and the ice in puddles cracks underfoot.

The ancients believed that even the stars and the planets sang, as they danced through their orbits. I wouldn't be surprised if this were true.

I suspect that, when the process of creation was finally finished, God not only looked at the earth, water, skies, birds of the air, and creeping and swimming things of every kind, and "saw that it was good." I think that God *listened* to the chorus of nature, which includes human singers like us, and *heard* that it was good as well.

———————— Contemplative Listening ————————

But the LORD answered her, "Martha, Martha, you are worried and distracted by many things; there is need of only one thing. Mary has chosen the better part, which will not be taken away from her."

(Luke 10:41)

Joining vigorously in the singing of hymns and service music, whether in choir, clergy stalls, or congregation, has always given me a great deal of pleasure. But I have a confession to make: some of my most profound moments of an awareness of God have occurred when I have not sung at all, but listened with all my heart and soul to the music of others.

I remember sitting with my husband in a wooden pew in the back row of the choir stalls at the immense Cathedral of St. John the Divine in New York City. We listened to and felt (because we were sitting right below the organ pipes) the mystery of the Trinity in a more profound way than in any sermon, as the organist played the French composer Olivier Messaien's "Meditations on the Holy Trinity." I remember attending our first Evensong at Kings College Chapel in Cambridge,

England, when the boys' voices, soaring into that incredible fan vaulting, brought us so close to heaven that we were both in tears. I remember our spiritual exhilaration one Sunday at the Augustinerkirche in Vienna, when the music of the Schubert Mass in A-flat major, with orchestra and choir, gave us a foretaste of the worship of the "Angels and Archangels and … all the company of heaven."

During all of those moments, I seemed to be doing nothing. I seemed to be a passive member of the congregation. But appearances were deceiving. My silence made it possible to listen with the kind of focus that deepened my worship in an extraordinary way.

Those moments remind me of the story of the busy Martha, bustling around in the kitchen, who is annoyed at her sister Mary, sitting quietly at Jesus' feet, doing "nothing." Everybody who has ever had to prepare meals can sympathize; Jesus and Mary would have become ravenously hungry if it had not been for Martha's diligence. But Jesus tries to explain to Martha the importance of Mary's activity—the activity of contemplative listening. Both sisters have an important role.

Every once in a while, someone suggests that choirs who sing anthems or other parts of the service by themselves are taking away liturgical participation from the congregation. I think such a statement is based on a false understanding of liturgy: that the only way to participate in worship is the way of Martha, which is doing. Jesus's words to Martha remind us that being is an important activity, too.

The Martha work of the choir gives the congregation the space to just be, providing them with a rich spiritual opportunity. They are not excluded when you sing any more than they are excluded when the priest prays the Eucharistic Prayer. Instead, they have joined inwardly in your music, and, in their silence—the silence of the listening Mary— have drawn closer to God.

———— The Communion of Saints ————

Who are these like stars appearing, these, before God's throne who stand?

(Hymn 286, The Hymnal 1982)

I learned in Sunday school that prayer is talking with God. Although I have discovered since then that prayer can also be many other things, I continue to reach out to God through words. Sometimes they are my own, but occasionally, especially in times of spiritual dryness or in crisis, it is a blessing to join a greater chorus of prayer.

I am grateful for The Book of Common Prayer, which contains within its covers Morning, Noonday, and Evening Prayer; Compline; Daily Devotions for Individuals and Families; all the Psalms; and a wonderful collection of Prayers and Thanksgivings. I find the prayer books of other denominations and collections such as *The Oxford Book of Prayer* invaluable and inspiring resources. But there is another prayer resource that most of us do not recognize, because we are singing it! It is the prayer embedded in the texts of our hymns and anthems.

As I turn the pages of the hymnal, I can pray with many companions from every era of Christian history. I stand beside one of the earliest Christian communities around the eucharistic table, as I sing "Father, we thank thee who hast planted," knowing that both those courageous early followers of the Way and we who celebrate the eucharist now are part of one bread, kneaded from the grain scattered on the hillsides across the world and throughout the centuries. I can protect myself with the shield of the Holy Trinity like St. Patrick of Ireland, when he composed "I Bind unto Myself Today" to ward off an attack by a Druidic chief.

I express my longing for Jesus Christ with the great "'O' Antiphons," traditionally sung in monasteries in late Advent since the eighth century. I celebrate creation with St. Francis in "All Creatures of our God and King." I sense the awe that inspired Thomas Aquinas to write "Now My Tongue the Mystery Telling" and imbibe some of the courage of Martin Luther when I pray, "A Mighty Fortress Is Our God." I find comfort by joining with the martyr Dietrich Bonhoeffer in his Nazi prison cell, "by gracious powers so wonderfully sheltered." [7]

I pray in the company of poets: George Herbert, John Donne,

Robert Bridges, Christina Rossetti, W. H. Auden. I join in the prayer of many cultures as I sing "Jesu, Jesu, fill us with your love" or "Many and great, O God, are thy works." The words of our music remind me that I never pray alone, but that my prayer joins those of Christians who have gone before me and of those who still surround me, all the company of heaven.

—————————— Contemplation ——————————

Lost in wonder, love, and praise.

(Hymn 657, The Hymnal 1982)

Have you ever found that you cannot silence the insistent memory of certain fragments of music you have been singing in the choir? It is as if an internal tape recorder is with you throughout the day, sometimes half-forgotten and sometimes playing at full volume. Instead of resisting this inner music—"I can't get that anthem out of my mind!"—we can let it teach us a very ancient way to pray.

That fragment of melody can become a focus for contemplative prayer or centering prayer, the wordless prayer in which we just focus on God's presence. When I first discovered this type of prayer, it felt as if, after driving in heavy traffic through busy streets, I had finally emerged into the fresh air and peacefulness of a secluded ocean cove. As life goes on, I depend more and more on this kind of prayer time, during which I try to quiet the continual buzz of my own thoughts in order to focus on God. Of course, that is more easily said than done.

Many teachers advise silently repeating a word or phrase (often called a "mantra") along with the rhythm of the breath as a helpful way to calm the clamor of our minds. One of them, an anonymous fourteenth-century monk, calls this method "shooting a dart of longing love" toward God.

When I have a melodic phrase running through my head and take time from my busy life to spend at least ten to fifteen minutes in quiet, I discover that the music can become a mantra—a dart of longing love—helping me to keep my attention turned toward God. I just hold the mantra in my mind as I breathe in time with the rhythm of the music, or I might choose to chant it out loud.

A fine source for this kind of prayer is the evocative chant of the Taizé community in France. Long after I have been singing Taizé chant, it continues to calm me as I hear it in my inner ear.

But phrases of hymns and anthems often have the same haunting quality. Perhaps it is "Let all mortal flesh keep silence," reminding me to put into God's hands both soul and body in quiet prayer. When I feel isolated and alone, it might be "Lord Jesus, think on me." A joyous

"Alleluia" might express a time of happiness; "Come, Holy Ghost, our souls inspire" will call on God's guidance and support. Perhaps, I even choose "lost in wonder, love, and praise," which is both a mantra and a perfect description of contemplative prayer itself.

—————————— Change ——————————

For the present form of this world is passing away.
(1 Corinthians 7:31b)

When Paul wrote this to the church in Corinth, Christians expected that Jesus' return was imminent: Life in its present form would, indeed, "pass away." Almost two thousand years later, however, these lines continue to ring true. "Present forms"—the things we are accustomed to—indeed seem to be passing away at a rapid and often disturbing rate. One way to deal with this is to cling tenaciously to what is familiar, resisting change with all our might. Another way is to acknowledge that, although change is often difficult, it helps us to grow, especially if we know that beyond all the "changes and chances of this mortal life" (The Book of Common Prayer, 1928) is the unchangeable love of God.

Changes in the words and music of our worship raise all kinds of anxiety in us. I remember being so familiar with the 1928 Book of Common Prayer that I never needed to open it during a service. The series of trial liturgies, identified by the color or pattern of their covers, were disorienting, and the rich resources in the new prayer book took some getting used to.

The new emphases in the 1979 Book of Common Prayer required new hymnody, and many people held their breath when they opened *The Hymnal 1982*. Would their favorite hymns still be in there? If not, what new ones would replace them? It was a decade of excitement and anxiety, expectation and mourning.

These new books have become very familiar now. It is hard to believe that I haven't sung "Lift High the Cross," "All My Hope on God Is Founded," and "Be Thou My Vision" since childhood. I wonder what it was like in the fifteenth and sixteenth centuries, when people who were accustomed to hearing plainsong in church were suddenly expected to sing the psalm tunes of the Reformation, or in the eighteenth century, when people as various as Wolfgang Amadeus Mozart, Isaac Watts, and Charles Wesley wrote daring new music for the church.

Perhaps getting used to new hymns is good practice for getting used to the other changes in our lives, for change is inevitable: We grow, we age, we die, and so do the people we love most. Our favorite priest is called to another parish, or our beloved organist retires. Our children become adults and move away. Just when we think we have control of our lives, something happens to show us that the future is not in our hands.

Our hymnal holds within its covers the melodies from many centuries that have proven to be of lasting worth. Perhaps we are like living hymnals. Nothing of value in our lives really disappears. We contain within our souls all the events and all the seasons of our lives—childhood, youth, maturity. The unchanging God's constant and loving grace binds all of these changes, perhaps especially those that we have most resisted, into one book, containing both the old songs and the new.

———————— Heaven's Door ————————

I had heard of you by the hearing of the ear, but now my eye sees you.

(Job 42:5)

In a poem entitled "Church-musick," the English poet and priest George Herbert writes, "But if I travell in your companie, You know the way to heavens doore." We who also travel in the company of church music know that Herbert was right.

The worship of our remote ancestors gave birth to all the arts. Music, dance, and the visual arts were first of all sacred exercises, the human response to the numinous. And today music continues to be an integral part of our worship, for it opens us—heart, mind, body, and spirit—to God. My friend Steven has long studied the relationship of music with liturgy and has told me that he thinks that it becomes "heaven's door" in a variety of ways.

Music sets words apart, rather like a "consecration of the sonic world." It strengthens the emotional content of the liturgy. It echoes the order of the cosmos and unifies our worship. And finally, in Steven's words, it gives us knowledge of God "in whose creative play the singing worshipper can claim a share." [8]

I love the idea of God's creative play. It makes me think that, even though the derivation of the word "liturgy" suggests that it is "the work of the people," perhaps considering it "the play of the people" would be more accurate. The child psychologist Jean Piaget called child's play "the herald of the arts." When we were young children, our play was like a door through which we investigated the amazing world into which we had been born. Now that we are adults, the arts are the door through which we glimpse most vividly the world within us and beyond us. And both of those worlds are unseen; they are mystery. We can't see that part of us we call our heart or soul, but that part of us is definitely there, controlling the way we feel, the way we think, and the way we act.

And we can't see God. We don't have videotapes of Jesus' life or recordings of the Sermon on the Mount. No spaceship can reach the Creator's dwelling; no scientific instrument can measure the power of the Spirit. We need another way to know God, another "doore."

I remember a wonderful conversation I once had with a beautiful young woman, a cellist raised in a nonreligious household, who told me, "I can't understand how anyone who loves music could not feel the presence of something beyond us."

I think that the door that is opened by music is the door to our inmost selves, and that God is always waiting there for the door to open. When we sing, we not only begin to open this door within ourselves, but also enable those who hear us to open it within themselves. What greater blessing, what greater privilege, could God give us in our ministry as choir singers?

———————————— **Prayers** ————————————

Bless, O Lord, those who sing in your church. Grant that what we sing with our lips we may believe in our hearts, and that what we believe in our hearts we may show forth in our lives, through Jesus Christ our Lord. Amen.

Almighty God, you have made us so that our hearts are moved by music and our minds attuned through sacred harmonies to the understanding of your divine mysteries: grant, we pray, that all who in this church unite in making to you an offering of music may know ourselves to be your ministers, and that the hearts of those who hear may be uplifted and strengthened in their faith and hope in you; through Jesus Christ our Lord. Amen.[9]

Anonymous

Praise to the Trinity!
You are music and life,
Source and creator of all that is.
Praised by angelic hosts,
You shine in secret splendor,
Beyond human understanding;
And yet, you are the life of all.

Hildegard of Bingen, 12th c.[10]

O Lord our God, who gives ear to the praises of your church on earth and before whom the heavens bow and adore: look, we beseech you, upon those who sing in this choir; give us reverence in worship, sincerity of purpose, and purity of life; that what we sing with our lips may be the sacrifice of our hearts; to the honor and glory of your holy name. Amen.[11]

Anonymous

Let all the world in ev'ry corner sing,
    My God and King.
The heavens are not too high,
His praise may thither flie.
The earth is not too low,
His praises there may grow.

Let all the world in ev'ry corner sing,
    My God and King.
The church with psalms must shout,
No doore can keep them out;
But, above all, the heart
Must bear the longest part.

Let all the world in ev'ry corner sing,
    My God and King.

George Herbert

O Lord Jesus Christ, who before your Passion joined with your disciples in a hymn of praise: grant, we beseech you, to those who offer the sacrifice of song in your church that we may one day join in the music of your church in heaven, and adore you for ever; to whom with the Father and the Holy Spirit be all honor and glory, world without end. Amen.[12]

As used at Salisbury

Teach me, Lord, to sing of your mercies. Turn my soul into a garden, where the flowers dance in the gentle breeze, praising you with their beauty. Let my soul be filled with beautiful virtues; let me be inspired by your Holy Spirit; let me praise you always.

St. Teresa of Avila

O God, whom saints and angels delight to worship in heaven: Be ever present with your servants who seek through art and music to perfect the praises offered by your people on earth; and grant to us even now glimpses of your beauty, and make us worthy at length to behold it unveiled for evermore; through Jesus Christ our Lord. Amen.

The Book of Common Prayer[13]

It is a good thing to give thanks to the LORD,
    and to sing praises to your Name, O Most High;
To tell of your loving-kindness early in the morning
    and of your faithfulness in the night season;
On the psaltery, and on the lyre,
    and to the melody of the harp.
For you have made me glad by your acts, O LORD;
    and I shout for joy because of the works of your hands.

Psalm 92:1–4

What wondrous love is this,
O my soul, O my soul!
What wondrous love is this, O my soul!
What wondrous love is this
that caused the Lord of bliss
To lay aside his crown for my soul, for my soul,
To lay aside his crown for my soul.

To God and to the Lamb,
I will sing, I will sing,
To God and to the Lamb, I will sing.
To God and to the Lamb
who is the great I AM,
while millions join the theme, I will sing, I will sing,
while millions join the theme, I will sing.

And when from death I'm free,
I'll sing on, I'll sing on,
And when from death I'm free, I'll sing on;
And when from death I'm free
I'll sing and joyful be,
and through eternity I'll sing on, I'll sing on,
and through eternity I'll sing on.

American folk hymn, ca. 1835

Almighty God, who has given to us power to invent for ourselves songs and musical instruments and the skill to sound forth your praise: grant that the music heard in this your holy house may kindle a spirit of devotion in us your servants; and that we, taking our part in your prayer and praise here on earth, may hereafter join in the everlasting song of the redeemed around your throne; through Jesus Christ our Lord. Amen.[14]

As used at Salisbury

Bring us, O Lord God, at our last awakening into the house and gate of heaven, to enter into that gate and dwell in that house, where there shall be no darkness nor dazzling, but one equal light; no noise nor silence, but one equal music; no fears nor hopes, but one equal possession; no ends nor beginnings, but one equal eternity; in the habitations of Thy glory and dominion world without end.

John Donne

Notes

1. Quoted in Alice Parker, *Melodious Accord* (Chicago: Liturgy Training Publications, 1991), p. 29.

2. *Ibid.*

3. Hildegard of Bingen, *Book of Divine Works* (Santa Fe, NM: Bear & Co., Inc., 1987), p. 359.

4. Don Campbell, *The Mozart Effect* (New York: Avon Books, 1997), p. 14.

5. Quoted in *A Sourcebook about Music* (Chicago: Liturgy Training Publications, 1997), p. 6.

6. Linda Richer, ed., *Chatter with the Angels* (Chicago: GIA, 1999).

7. If you would like to know more background, *The Hymnal 1982 Companion* (Church Hymnal Corporation) is a helpful resource, as well as *A Closer Walk: Meditating on the Hymns for Year A*, by Nancy Roth (Church Publishing, 1998), the first of a series of meditations on hymn texts.

8. Steven Plank, *"The Way to Heavens Doore"* (Metuchen, NJ: The Scarecrow Press, Inc., 1994), p. 7.

9. Adapted from Frederick B. MacNutt, ed., *The Prayer Manual* (London: A.R. Mowbray & Co., Ltd., 1951), p. 163.

10. Free translation from the Latin by Nancy Roth.

11. Adapted from MacNutt, p. 163.

12. *Ibid.*, p. 162.

13. *The Book of Common Prayer* (New York: The Church Hymnal Corporation, 1979), p. 819, altered.

14. Adapted from MacNutt, p. 162.